The Roadmap to AI Mastery: A Guide to Building and Scaling Projects

Somdip Dey

Published by Somdip Dey, 2023.

About the author

Somdip Dey, FRSA

SOMDIP DEY, FRSA, ALSO professionally known as InteliDey, is an Embedded Artificial Intelligence scientist, engineer, entrepreneur, AI art & music creator and TED speaker. Dey is the CEO of Nosh Technologies, the CTO of Blockway Technologies and a Lecturer at the University of Essex, UK. He is also the Danah Zohar Professor of Quantum Philosophy & Professor of Practice (AI/ML) at Woxsen University, India. He has more than 13 years of industrial experience including working for Microsoft and Samsung in developing numerous technological products that are currently used by billions of people in different ways. For contributions to improving society through applications of embedded machine learning Dey is elected a Life Fellow of the Royal Society of Arts, named an MIT Innovator Under 35, an Outstanding Achiever in Education, Science &

Innovation at the 2023 India UK Achievers Honours and a 2022 World IP Review Leader. He is also a member of the Forbes Technology Council and regularly appears in news including Forbes, Entrepreneur, Business Insider, Tech Crunch and many more.

Table of Contents

Prologue 1
Chapter 1: Understanding the Fundamentals of AI: An Introduction to Key Concepts 3
Chapter 2: Laying the Foundation: Preparing Your Data for AI Projects 6
Chapter 2: Laying the Foundation: Preparing Your Data for AI Projects 9
Chapter 3: Choosing the Right Framework: A Guide to AI Model Selection 13
Chapter 4: Creating Your First AI Model: A Step-by-Step Tutorial 16
Chapter 5: Navigating AI Ethics: Ensuring Fairness and Transparency in Your Projects 19
Chapter 6: Building an AI-Powered Business: Identifying Opportunities for AI Implementation 22
Chapter 7: Overcoming Common AI Challenges: Troubleshooting and Optimization Strategies 25
Chapter 8: Scaling Your AI Projects: Infrastructure, Deployment, and Maintenance 28
Chapter 9: Collaborating in AI: Strategies for Cross-Functional Teams and Stakeholders 31
Chapter 10: The Future of AI: Emerging Technologies and Trends to Watch 34
Chapter 11: What is Deep Reinforcement Learning and How Can It Be Used in Projects? 37
Chapter 12: What is Explainable AI and How Can It Be Used in Projects? 40
Chapter 13: What is Federated Learning and How Can It Be Used in Projects? 43
Chapter 14: What is Generative Adversarial Networks and How Can It Be Used in Projects? 46
Chapter 15: What is Edge Computing and How Can It Be Used in Projects? 49

Chapter 16: What is Embedded Machine Learning and How is it Different from Federated Learning?..............................52
Chapter 17: How AI can be used to promote Environmental, Social, and Corporate Governance (ESG)............................55
Chapter 18: How AI can be used to promote Environmental Sustainability 58
Bonus Chapter: How to Communicate Effectively with Technical People in AI 61
Bonus Chapter: How to Communicate Effectively with Non-Technical People About AI Projects 64
Thank You for Reading 67
Connect with the author..69

Prologue

Welcome to "The Roadmap to AI Mastery: A Guide to Building and Scaling Projects." This book is designed for project managers, product managers and enthusiasts with a non-technical background in AI who are looking to gain foundational knowledge on how to build and scale AI projects for their companies.

AI has the potential to transform industries, improve processes, and drive business growth. However, many organizations struggle to understand how to leverage AI effectively, and the complex nature of the technology can make it difficult for non-technical professionals to know where to begin.

That's where this book comes in. Our goal is to provide you with a clear, practical guide to building and scaling AI projects, using real-world examples and friendly, approachable language. We'll cover everything from the fundamentals of AI to selecting the right framework, creating AI models, overcoming common challenges, and more.

We want to emphasize that this book is not a technical manual for AI experts. Instead, it serves as a starting point for non-technical professionals who are new to the world of AI and want to gain a foundational understanding of how it works and how it can be used in their organizations.

We believe that AI should be accessible and approachable for everyone, regardless of technical expertise. That's why we've written this book in a friendly tone, using real-world examples and practical advice to make AI more understandable and relatable.

By the end of this book, we hope that you'll have a better understanding of how AI works and how it can be used to meet your organization's business goals. We hope that this knowledge will give you the confidence to explore and experiment with AI, and to begin building successful AI projects that drive growth and innovation for your company.

So, let's get started on our journey to AI mastery. Thank you for joining us, and we hope you find this book informative and helpful in your quest to build and scale AI projects.

Chapter 1: Understanding the Fundamentals of AI: An Introduction to Key Concepts

Welcome to the world of artificial intelligence (AI)! In this chapter, we'll explore the basics of AI and the key concepts you need to understand before embarking on an AI project. Whether you're a beginner or an experienced professional, this chapter will provide a solid foundation for your AI journey.

What is AI?

Artificial intelligence (AI) refers to the ability of machines to perform tasks that typically require human intelligence, such as learning, reasoning, problem-solving, perception, and natural language processing. AI can be divided into two broad categories: narrow or weak AI and general or strong AI. Narrow AI refers to AI that is designed to perform specific tasks, such as playing chess or recognizing images. General AI, on the other hand, refers to AI that can perform any intellectual task that a human can.

Machine Learning

Machine learning is a subfield of AI that involves training machines to recognize patterns and make predictions based on data. There are three types of machine learning: supervised learning, unsupervised learning, and reinforcement learning. Supervised learning involves training a machine on a labeled dataset, while unsupervised learning involves training a machine on an unlabeled dataset. Reinforcement learning involves training a machine to make decisions based on rewards and punishments.

Deep Learning

Deep learning is a subset of machine learning that involves training artificial neural networks to recognize patterns and make predictions. Deep learning has been particularly successful in computer vision and natural language processing applications. A neural network is a set of algorithms modeled after the structure and function of the human brain. Neural networks are used in deep learning and can be trained to recognize patterns and make predictions.

Neural Networks

Neural networks are a type of machine learning algorithm that are modeled after the structure and function of the human brain. Neural networks consist of layers of interconnected nodes or neurons, which process and transmit information. Neural networks are used in deep learning and can be trained to recognize patterns and make predictions.

Data

Data is the lifeblood of AI. AI models require large amounts of high-quality data to be effective. Data can come in various forms, such as structured data (e.g., data stored in a database) and unstructured data (e.g., text, images, and video). Before training an AI model, it's important to preprocess the data to ensure it's clean, consistent, and in the right format.

Ethics

AI has the potential to impact society in profound ways, and it's essential to consider ethical implications when developing AI systems. AI ethics involves ensuring that AI systems are designed and deployed in a way that is fair, transparent, and accountable. Examples of ethical considerations in AI include ensuring that the data used to train AI models is representative and unbiased, and that AI systems are not used to perpetuate discrimination or violate privacy rights.

Conclusion

In this chapter, we've covered the fundamental concepts of AI, including the definition of AI, its subfields, such as machine learning and deep learning, and the importance of data and ethical considerations in AI development. As you embark on your AI journey, keep in mind that AI is a rapidly evolving field, and there is always more to learn. In the next chapter, we will dive deeper into preparing data for AI projects.

Chapter 2: Laying the Foundation: Preparing Your Data for AI Projects

Welcome to Chapter 2 of "The Roadmap to AI Mastery: A Guide to Building and Scaling Projects." In this chapter, we'll explore the critical step of preparing data for AI projects. Data is the lifeblood of AI, and without high-quality, clean data, your AI models will not perform effectively.

Understanding Your Data

The first step in preparing your data for AI projects is understanding your data. Data can come in many forms, such as structured data (e.g., data stored in a database) and unstructured data (e.g., text, images, and video). It's important to understand the type of data you have, its format, and its quality.

Data Cleaning

Once you have a good understanding of your data, the next step is data cleaning. Data cleaning involves identifying and correcting errors in the data, such as missing values, inconsistent values, and outliers. Data cleaning is a critical step in ensuring that your AI models are trained on high-quality data.

Data Preprocessing

After data cleaning, the next step is data preprocessing. Data preprocessing involves transforming the data into a format that can be used by AI models. This can include tasks such as scaling, normalization, and feature extraction. Data preprocessing is a critical step in preparing your data for AI projects, as it can significantly impact the performance of your AI models.

Data Augmentation

Data augmentation is a technique used to increase the amount of data available for training AI models. Data augmentation involves creating new data by applying transformations to existing data. For example, in image classification, data augmentation can involve flipping, rotating, or cropping images. Data augmentation is an effective way to improve the performance of AI models, especially when working with limited amounts of data.

Data Labelling

Data labelling involves assigning labels to data, such as identifying objects in an image or categorizing text. Data labelling is a critical step in supervised learning, as it provides the ground truth or correct answers that AI models use to learn. Data labelling can be done manually or with the help of automated tools.

Data Storage and Management

Finally, it's essential to store and manage your data effectively. As AI projects require large amounts of data, it's critical to have a system for storing and accessing data. This can include databases, cloud storage, or other data management systems. It's also important to have a system for version control, to keep track of changes to the data and ensure that you are working with the latest version.

Conclusion

In this chapter, we've covered the critical step of preparing data for AI projects. From understanding your data to cleaning, preprocessing, augmenting, labeling, and storing your data, we hope you have gained a solid understanding of how to lay the foundation for your AI projects. In the next chapter, we will explore choosing the right framework for your AI models.

Chapter 2: Laying the Foundation: Preparing Your Data for AI Projects

Welcome to Chapter 2 of "The Roadmap to AI Mastery: A Guide to Building and Scaling Projects." In this chapter, we'll explore the critical step of preparing data for AI projects. Data is the lifeblood of AI, and without high-quality, clean data, your AI models will not perform effectively.

Understanding Your Data

The first step in preparing your data for AI projects is understanding your data. Data can come in many forms, such as structured data (e.g., data stored in a database) and unstructured data (e.g., text, images, and video). Before you start preparing your data, you need to have a good understanding of the type of data you have, its format, and its quality.

For example, if you're working on a natural language processing project, you need to understand the format of the text data you're working with. Is it in plain text format or in HTML format? Does the data contain any special characters or symbols that need to be removed or replaced?

Data Cleaning

Once you have a good understanding of your data, the next step is data cleaning. Data cleaning involves identifying and correcting errors in the data, such as missing values, inconsistent values, and outliers. Data cleaning is a critical step in ensuring that your AI models are trained on high-quality data.

For example, if you're working on an image recognition project, you may need to remove images that are low quality or contain irrelevant objects. If you're working on a natural language processing project, you may need to remove stop words or correct spelling errors in the text data.

Data Preprocessing

After data cleaning, the next step is data preprocessing. Data preprocessing involves transforming the data into a format that can be used by AI models. This can include tasks such as scaling, normalization, and feature extraction. Data preprocessing is a critical step in preparing your data for AI projects, as it can significantly impact the performance of your AI models.

For example, in an image classification project, you may need to resize images to a standard size or convert them to grayscale. In a natural language processing project, you may need to tokenize the text data or convert it to a numerical representation.

Data Augmentation

Data augmentation is a technique used to increase the amount of data available for training AI models. Data augmentation involves creating new data by applying transformations to existing data. For example, in image classification, data augmentation can involve flipping, rotating, or cropping images. Data augmentation is an effective way to improve the performance of AI models, especially when working with limited amounts of data.

For example, in a facial recognition project, you may use data augmentation techniques such as flipping, rotating, and changing the lighting of images to increase the size of your training dataset.

Data Labelling

Data labelling involves assigning labels to data, such as identifying objects in an image or categorizing text. Data labelling is a critical step in supervised learning, as it provides the ground truth or correct answers that AI models use to learn. Data labelling can be done manually or with the help of automated tools.

For example, in a sentiment analysis project, you may manually label text data as positive, negative, or neutral. In an object detection project, you may use automated tools to label objects in images.

Data Storage and Management

Finally, it's essential to store and manage your data effectively. As AI projects require large amounts of data, it's critical to have a system for storing and accessing data. This can include databases, cloud storage, or other data management systems. It's also important to have a system for version control, to keep track of changes to the data and ensure that you are working with the latest version.

For example, if you're working on a deep learning project that involves training a neural network on a large dataset of images, you may need to store your data in a cloud-based storage system such as Amazon S3 or Google Cloud Storage. This will allow you to easily access and manipulate your data without worrying about storage limitations on your local machine.

Version control is also critical in data management. As you make changes to your data, you need to ensure that you are working with the latest version. Version control systems such as Git allow you to track changes to your data and collaborate with other team members.

Conclusion

In this chapter, we've covered the critical step of preparing data for AI projects. From understanding your data to cleaning, preprocessing, augmenting, labeling, and storing your data, we hope you have gained a solid understanding of how to lay the foundation for your AI projects.

Remember, the quality of your data is crucial to the performance of your AI models. Take the time to understand your data, clean it thoroughly, and preprocess it effectively. Use data augmentation to increase your dataset and label your data carefully to ensure your models are trained on accurate information. Finally, store and manage your data properly to ensure that you are working with the latest version.

In the next chapter, we will explore choosing the right framework for your AI models.

Chapter 3: Choosing the Right Framework: A Guide to AI Model Selection

Welcome to Chapter 3 of "The Roadmap to AI Mastery: A Guide to Building and Scaling Projects." In this chapter, we'll explore the critical step of choosing the right framework for your AI models. There are many frameworks available for building AI models, and selecting the right one can significantly impact the performance and scalability of your models.

Understanding AI Frameworks

AI frameworks are software tools that provide a library of pre-built algorithms and functions to make building AI models easier. Frameworks can handle tasks such as data preprocessing, model training, and model evaluation. Some of the most popular AI frameworks include TensorFlow, PyTorch, and Keras.

Choosing the Right Framework

When choosing a framework, there are several factors to consider, including the complexity of your project, the size of your dataset, and the skill level of your team.

For example, if you're working on a simple image classification project with a small dataset, Keras may be a good choice. Keras is a user-friendly framework that's easy to learn and provides a high-level API for building AI models. On the other hand, if you're working on a complex natural language processing project with a large dataset, TensorFlow may be a better choice. TensorFlow provides more advanced features for building complex models and can handle large amounts of data.

Here are some other factors to consider when selecting a framework:

1. ***Community Support***: A framework with a large community of developers can provide access to helpful resources and support.
2. ***Performance***: Some frameworks are optimized for specific hardware or architectures, which can significantly impact the performance of your models.
3. ***Scalability***: Consider the scalability of the framework, especially if you plan to work with large datasets or train models on multiple machines.
4. ***Learning Curve***: Consider the skill level of your team and the ease of learning the framework.

For example, PyTorch is known for its ease of use and can be learned quickly, making it a great choice for small teams with limited experience in AI. On the other hand, frameworks such as TensorFlow and Theano have a steeper learning curve but provide more advanced features for building complex models.

Framework Examples

Here are some examples of frameworks and their typical use cases:

1. ***TensorFlow***: TensorFlow is a popular framework for building deep learning models and is widely used in image and speech recognition, natural language processing, and robotics.

2. ***PyTorch***: PyTorch is a popular choice for building deep learning models and is commonly used in natural language processing, computer vision, and reinforcement learning.
3. ***Keras***: Keras is a high-level API built on top of TensorFlow and is popular for building deep learning models in image classification and natural language processing.
4. ***Theano***: Theano is a deep learning framework known for its fast computation and is used in image and speech recognition, natural language processing, and robotics.

Conclusion

In this chapter, we've covered the critical step of selecting the right framework for your AI models. We've discussed the factors to consider when choosing a framework, such as the complexity of your project, the size of your dataset, and the skill level of your team. We've also provided examples of popular frameworks and their typical use cases.

Remember, selecting the right framework can significantly impact the performance and scalability of your models. Take the time to understand the strengths and weaknesses of each framework and select the one that best fits your project's requirements. In the next chapter, we will explore the process of building and training AI models.

Chapter 4: Creating Your First AI Model: A Step-by-Step Tutorial

Welcome to Chapter 4 of "The Roadmap to AI Mastery: A Guide to Building and Scaling Projects." In this chapter, we'll walk you through the process of creating your first AI model, step by step.

Before we get started, it's important to note that building an AI model requires a good understanding of programming concepts and AI fundamentals. If you're new to programming or AI, we recommend reviewing Chapters 1-3 before proceeding.

Step 1: Selecting Your Problem

The first step in creating your AI model is selecting your problem. What do you want your AI model to accomplish? Do you want it to classify images, generate text, or predict stock prices?

For this tutorial, let's create a simple image classification model that can distinguish between cats and dogs.

Step 2: Collecting and Preprocessing Data

The next step is collecting and preprocessing your data. You'll need a dataset of images of cats and dogs to train your model. You can use publicly available datasets, such as the CIFAR-10 dataset or the ImageNet dataset, or create your own dataset.

Once you have your dataset, you'll need to preprocess it. This involves resizing the images to a standard size and converting them to a numerical format that can be used by your model. You may also need to perform data augmentation techniques, such as flipping and rotating images, to increase the size of your dataset.

Step 3: Building Your Model

Now it's time to build your model. There are many different types of AI models, such as convolutional neural networks (CNNs) and recurrent neural networks (RNNs). For this tutorial, we'll use a simple CNN.

Your CNN will consist of several layers, such as convolutional layers, pooling layers, and fully connected layers. Each layer performs a specific operation on the input data, such as extracting features or reducing the size of the data.

Step 4: Training Your Model

Once you've built your model, it's time to train it. Training involves feeding your model with your preprocessed data and adjusting the weights of the model to minimize the error or loss function.

During training, you'll need to specify hyperparameters, such as the learning rate and the number of epochs. The learning rate determines how quickly your model adjusts its weights, while the number of epochs determines how many times your model will see the entire dataset.

Step 5: Evaluating Your Model

After training your model, it's important to evaluate its performance. You can do this by testing your model on a set of images that it has not seen before and comparing its predictions to the ground truth or correct labels.

You can also use metrics, such as accuracy and precision, to measure the performance of your model. Accuracy measures the percentage of correctly classified images, while precision measures the percentage of correctly classified images out of all the images that were classified as a certain class.

Step 6: Improving Your Model

Finally, you can improve your model by making adjustments based on its performance. For example, you can adjust the hyperparameters, such as the learning rate and the number of epochs, to improve accuracy. You can also add more layers to your CNN or try a different type of AI model.

Conclusion

In this chapter, we've walked you through the process of creating your first AI model, step by step. We've covered selecting your problem, collecting and preprocessing data, building your model, training your model, evaluating your model, and improving your model.

Remember, building AI models requires patience and practice. Don't be discouraged if your first model doesn't perform as well as you hoped. Take the time to experiment with different approaches and learn from your mistakes.

Chapter 5: Navigating AI Ethics: Ensuring Fairness and Transparency in Your Projects

Welcome to Chapter 5 of "The Roadmap to AI Mastery: A Guide to Building and Scaling Projects." In this chapter, we'll explore the critical topic of AI ethics and how to ensure fairness and transparency in your AI projects.

As AI becomes more prevalent in our daily lives, it's essential to consider the ethical implications of its use. AI models can perpetuate biases and discrimination if not designed and implemented carefully.

Understanding AI Ethics

AI ethics involves the principles and guidelines that govern the use and development of AI systems. These principles aim to ensure that AI is used in an ethical and responsible manner, with a focus on fairness, transparency, accountability, and privacy.

Some of the key principles of AI ethics include:

1. *Fairness*: AI systems should not discriminate against any group or individual.
2. *Transparency*: AI systems should be transparent in their decision-making processes and provide explanations for their outputs.
3. *Accountability*: Individuals and organizations responsible for the development and use of AI systems should be held accountable for their actions.

4. ***Privacy***: AI systems should respect individuals' privacy and protect their personal information.

Ensuring Fairness in Your AI Projects

To ensure fairness in your AI projects, it's essential to understand the potential biases that can be present in your data and AI models. Biases can arise from a variety of sources, including historical data, sampling bias, and algorithmic bias.

For example, if you're building an AI model to predict creditworthiness, historical data that includes discriminatory lending practices can perpetuate biases in your model. To address this, you can use techniques such as data anonymization, data balancing, and fairness metrics to ensure that your model is fair and unbiased.

Ensuring Transparency in Your AI Projects

To ensure transparency in your AI projects, it's important to provide explanations for your model's outputs. This can involve providing insights into the decision-making processes of your model, such as which features were most influential in making a prediction.

For example, if you're building an AI model to predict disease outcomes, providing explanations for your model's predictions can help healthcare professionals understand how the model arrived at its conclusions and make informed decisions.

Ensuring Accountability in Your AI Projects

To ensure accountability in your AI projects, it's important to have a system in place for tracking and monitoring the development and use of your AI models. This can involve setting up a framework for ethical decision-making, establishing a code of ethics, and having clear guidelines for the use of AI models.

For example, if you're building an AI model to make hiring decisions, you can establish a code of ethics that ensures the model is fair and unbiased in its decision-making processes. You can also have a system in place for monitoring the model's performance and identifying any potential biases.

Conclusion

In this chapter, we've explored the critical topic of AI ethics and how to ensure fairness and transparency in your AI projects. We've discussed the key principles of AI ethics, such as fairness, transparency, accountability, and privacy, and provided examples of how to ensure these principles are upheld in your AI projects.

Remember, AI ethics is a constantly evolving field, and it's important to stay up to date with the latest guidelines and best practices. By prioritizing fairness, transparency, and accountability in your AI projects, you can help ensure that AI is used in an ethical and responsible manner. In the next chapter, we'll explore the process of deploying and scaling AI models.

Chapter 6: Building an AI-Powered Business: Identifying Opportunities for AI Implementation

Welcome to Chapter 6 of "The Roadmap to AI Mastery: A Guide to Building and Scaling Projects." In this chapter, we'll explore the topic of building an AI-powered business and how to identify opportunities for AI implementation.

As AI becomes more prevalent, businesses are starting to recognize the potential benefits of implementing AI systems. AI can help businesses improve efficiency, reduce costs, and gain a competitive advantage.

Identifying Opportunities for AI Implementation

The first step in building an AI-powered business is identifying opportunities for AI implementation. There are many areas of a business where AI can be applied, such as customer service, supply chain management, and marketing.

Here are some examples of how AI can be implemented in different areas of a business:

1. *Customer Service*: AI-powered chatbots can provide 24/7 customer support, handle routine inquiries, and free up customer service agents to handle more complex issues.
2. *Supply Chain Management*: AI can help optimize inventory levels, predict demand, and reduce waste

by identifying areas for improvement in the supply chain.
3. ***Marketing***: AI can help businesses personalize marketing campaigns, identify target audiences, and analyze customer behavior to improve conversion rates.
4. ***Finance***: AI can help businesses streamline financial processes, detect fraud, and analyze financial data to identify areas for improvement.

Assessing the Feasibility of AI Implementation

Once you've identified potential areas for AI implementation, it's important to assess the feasibility of implementation. This involves evaluating the resources required, such as data, hardware, and personnel, and determining the potential return on investment (ROI) of implementing AI.

For example, if you're considering implementing AI in customer service, you'll need to evaluate the amount and quality of data available, the hardware and software required to build an AI-powered chatbot, and the personnel required to develop and maintain the chatbot.

You'll also need to consider the potential ROI of implementing AI. Will implementing AI lead to cost savings, increased efficiency, or improved customer satisfaction? Answering these questions will help you determine whether AI implementation is feasible and worthwhile for your business.

Building an AI Strategy

Once you've identified opportunities for AI implementation and assessed the feasibility of implementation, it's time to build an AI strategy. Your AI strategy should outline your goals for implementing AI, the resources required, and the timeline for implementation.

Your AI strategy should also consider the potential ethical implications of AI implementation and ensure that your AI systems are designed and implemented in an ethical and responsible manner.

Conclusion

In this chapter, we've explored the topic of building an AI-powered business and how to identify opportunities for AI implementation. We've discussed potential areas for AI implementation, such as customer service, supply chain management, marketing, and finance, and provided examples of how AI can be applied in these areas.

Remember, identifying opportunities for AI implementation and building an AI strategy requires careful consideration of the resources required and potential ROI of implementation. By prioritizing ethics and responsible implementation, businesses can build AI-powered systems that are efficient, effective, and ethical.

Chapter 7: Overcoming Common AI Challenges: Troubleshooting and Optimization Strategies

Welcome to Chapter 7 of "The Roadmap to AI Mastery: A Guide to Building and Scaling Projects." In this chapter, we'll explore the common challenges that arise in AI projects and provide strategies for troubleshooting and optimization.

AI projects can be complex, and even the most experienced developers can encounter challenges along the way. By understanding common challenges and knowing how to overcome them, you can ensure that your AI projects are successful and deliver the desired outcomes.

Common AI Challenges

Here are some of the common challenges that arise in AI projects:

- ***Data Quality***: The quality of your data can greatly impact the performance of your AI model. Poor quality data can lead to biases, errors, and inaccurate predictions.

For example, if you're building an AI model to predict sales, but your data contains incomplete or inaccurate information, your model may not perform well.

- **Overfitting**: Overfitting occurs when your model is too complex and fits the training data too well. This can result in poor performance on new, unseen data.

For example, if you're building an image classification model and your model performs well on the training data but poorly on new images, your model may be overfitting.

- **Underfitting**: Underfitting occurs when your model is too simple and cannot capture the underlying patterns in the data. This can result in poor performance on both the training data and new data.

For example, if you're building an AI model to predict customer churn and your model performs poorly on both the training data and new data, your model may be underfitting.

Strategies for Overcoming Common

AI Challenges Here are some strategies for overcoming common AI challenges:

- **Data Quality**: To address data quality issues, it's important to ensure that your data is clean, complete, and unbiased. This can involve data cleaning techniques, such as removing duplicates and outliers, and data augmentation techniques, such as synthesizing new data to increase the size of your dataset.
- **Overfitting**: To address overfitting, you can use techniques such as regularization, dropout, and early stopping. Regularization involves adding a penalty term to the loss function to reduce the complexity of the model, while dropout involves randomly dropping out some of the neurons in the model to prevent over-reliance on specific features. Early stopping involves

stopping the training process when the validation loss stops improving.
- *Underfitting*: To address underfitting, you can try using a more complex model or adding more features to your dataset. You can also experiment with different hyperparameters, such as the learning rate and batch size, to find the optimal values for your model.

Conclusion

In this chapter, we've explored the common challenges that arise in AI projects and provided strategies for troubleshooting and optimization. We've discussed the importance of data quality and provided examples of how to address data quality issues. We've also discussed overfitting and underfitting and provided strategies for addressing these issues.

Remember, building AI models requires patience, practice, and experimentation. Don't be discouraged if your model doesn't perform as well as you hoped. By understanding common challenges and knowing how to overcome them, you can ensure that your AI projects are successful and deliver the desired outcomes. In the next chapter, we'll explore the process of deploying and scaling AI models.

Chapter 8: Scaling Your AI Projects: Infrastructure, Deployment, and Maintenance

Welcome to Chapter 8 of "The Roadmap to AI Mastery: A Guide to Building and Scaling Projects." In this chapter, we'll explore the critical topic of scaling your AI projects and the infrastructure, deployment, and maintenance required to do so.

Scaling your AI projects involves taking your model from a proof of concept to a fully operational system that can handle real-world data and use cases. This requires careful planning and execution, and a focus on infrastructure, deployment, and maintenance.

Infrastructure for Scaling AI Projects

To scale your AI projects, it's essential to have a robust infrastructure that can handle the computational requirements of your model. This involves having access to powerful hardware and software, such as GPUs and deep learning frameworks.

Cloud-based infrastructure, such as Amazon Web Services (AWS) and Google Cloud Platform (GCP), can provide scalable, on-demand resources for AI projects. This allows you to easily scale your infrastructure as your model and data requirements grow.

Deployment for Scaling AI Projects

To deploy your AI model, you'll need to decide on the appropriate deployment method for your use case. This can involve deploying your model on-premises or in the cloud.

On-premises deployment involves running your model on local hardware, such as a server or workstation. This can provide more control and security over your model and data but can be limited by hardware constraints.

Cloud deployment involves running your model on cloud-based infrastructure, such as AWS or GCP. This can provide more flexibility and scalability but may require additional security measures to protect your data.

Maintenance for Scaling AI Projects

To ensure the continued performance and accuracy of your AI model, it's essential to have a maintenance plan in place. This can involve regular monitoring and updates to your model and infrastructure.

Regular monitoring involves tracking the performance of your model and identifying any issues or errors. This can involve using tools such as logging and metrics to track performance and identify potential issues.

Updates to your model and infrastructure can involve implementing new features, improving accuracy, and addressing any security vulnerabilities.

Conclusion

In this chapter, we've explored the critical topic of scaling your AI projects and the infrastructure, deployment, and maintenance required to do so. We've discussed the importance of having a robust infrastructure that can handle the computational requirements of your model and provided examples of cloud-based infrastructure options.

We've also discussed deployment methods, such as on-premises and cloud-based deployment, and the importance of having a maintenance plan in place to ensure the continued performance and accuracy of your model.

Remember, scaling your AI projects requires careful planning and execution. By focusing on infrastructure, deployment, and maintenance, you can ensure that your AI model is ready to handle real-world data and use cases.

Chapter 9: Collaborating in AI: Strategies for Cross-Functional Teams and Stakeholders

Welcome to Chapter 9 of "The Roadmap to AI Mastery: A Guide to Building and Scaling Projects." In this chapter, we'll explore the critical topic of collaborating in AI projects and strategies for working with cross-functional teams and stakeholders.

Collaboration is essential for the success of any AI project. AI projects involve a variety of stakeholders, including data scientists, developers, business analysts, and end-users. Effective collaboration requires clear communication, a shared understanding of goals and objectives, and a focus on delivering value to stakeholders.

Working with Cross-Functional Teams

Cross-functional teams are a key component of successful AI projects. Cross-functional teams bring together individuals with different skills and perspectives to collaborate on a common goal.

To work effectively with cross-functional teams, it's important to establish clear roles and responsibilities, foster a culture of collaboration, and provide opportunities for feedback and communication.

For example, if you're building an AI model to improve customer experience, your cross-functional team may include data scientists, developers, business analysts, and customer service representatives. Each team member should have a clear understanding of their role in the project and how their contributions will help achieve the project's goals.

Working with Stakeholders

Stakeholders are individuals or groups who have an interest in the outcome of your AI project. Stakeholders can include customers, business partners, investors, and regulatory bodies.

To work effectively with stakeholders, it's important to establish clear communication channels, involve stakeholders in the project, and provide regular updates on the project's progress.

For example, if you're building an AI model to improve supply chain management, your stakeholders may include suppliers, logistics providers, and regulatory bodies. It's important to involve these stakeholders in the project and provide regular updates on the project's progress to ensure that their needs and concerns are addressed.

Managing Expectations

Effective collaboration also requires managing stakeholder expectations. AI projects can be complex, and it's important to set realistic expectations for what can be achieved within a given timeframe and budget.

To manage stakeholder expectations, it's important to communicate the limitations and risks of the project, provide regular updates on progress, and manage changes in scope or requirements.

For example, if you're building an AI model to predict sales, it's important to communicate the limitations of the model and the potential risks of relying solely on the model's predictions. It's also important to provide regular updates on the model's performance and manage changes in the data or business environment that may impact the model's predictions.

Conclusion

In this chapter, we've explored the critical topic of collaborating in AI projects and strategies for working with cross-functional teams and stakeholders. We've discussed the importance of clear communication, a shared understanding of goals and objectives, and managing stakeholder expectations.

Remember, effective collaboration is essential for the success of any AI project. By working effectively with cross-functional teams and stakeholders, you can ensure that your AI projects deliver value to stakeholders and achieve their intended goals.

Chapter 10: The Future of AI: Emerging Technologies and Trends to Watch

Welcome to Chapter 10 of "The Roadmap to AI Mastery: A Guide to Building and Scaling Projects." In this chapter, we'll explore the exciting topic of the future of AI and the emerging technologies and trends to watch.

AI is a rapidly evolving field, and staying up to date with emerging technologies and trends is essential for staying ahead of the curve and leveraging the full potential of AI.

Emerging Technologies and Trends

Here are some of the emerging technologies and trends to watch in the field of AI:

1. *Deep Reinforcement Learning*: Deep reinforcement learning is a subfield of AI that combines deep learning with reinforcement learning. This approach has shown promise in complex tasks such as game playing and robotics.
2. *Explainable AI*: Explainable AI involves building AI systems that can explain their decision-making processes in a way that is understandable to humans. This is important for ensuring transparency and accountability in AI systems.
3. *Federated Learning*: Federated learning is a distributed machine learning approach that allows multiple parties to collaboratively train a model

without sharing their data. This can help address privacy concerns while still allowing for the development of accurate models.
4. **Generative Adversarial Networks**: Generative adversarial networks (GANs) are a type of neural network that can generate new data based on existing data. GANs have shown promise in fields such as art and music generation.
5. *Edge Computing*: Edge computing involves processing data on local devices rather than in the cloud. This can provide faster processing times and reduce the amount of data that needs to be transmitted over the network.

The Importance of Keeping Up with Emerging Technologies and Trends

Staying up to date with emerging technologies and trends is essential for leveraging the full potential of AI. By staying up to date, you can identify new opportunities for implementing AI, improve the accuracy and performance of your models, and stay ahead of the competition.

For example, if you're building an AI model for image recognition, staying up to date with emerging technologies such as GANs and deep reinforcement learning can help improve the accuracy and performance of your model.

Conclusion

In this chapter, we've explored the exciting topic of the future of AI and the emerging technologies and trends to watch. We've discussed the importance of staying up to date with emerging technologies and trends and provided examples of how staying up to date can improve the accuracy and performance of your AI models.

Remember, AI is a rapidly evolving field, and staying up to date is essential for staying ahead of the curve and leveraging the full potential of AI. By keeping an eye on emerging technologies and trends, you can ensure that your AI projects are successful and deliver the desired outcomes.

Chapter 11: What is Deep Reinforcement Learning and How Can It Be Used in Projects?

Welcome to Chapter 11 of "The Roadmap to AI Mastery: A Guide to Building and Scaling Projects." In this chapter, we'll explore the exciting field of deep reinforcement learning (DRL) and its applications in AI projects.

What is Deep Reinforcement Learning?

Deep reinforcement learning is a subfield of AI that combines deep learning with reinforcement learning. Reinforcement learning involves training an AI agent to learn from its environment by receiving rewards or punishments for specific actions.

Deep reinforcement learning involves using deep neural networks to learn complex relationships between actions, observations, and rewards. This approach has shown promise in complex tasks such as game playing and robotics.

How Can Deep Reinforcement Learning Be Used in Projects?

Deep reinforcement learning can be used in a wide range of AI projects, including:

1. **Robotics**: Deep reinforcement learning can be used to train robots to perform complex tasks such as grasping objects and navigating environments.

2. **Gaming**: Deep reinforcement learning has been used to train AI agents to play complex games such as Go and Chess.
3. **Self-Driving Cars**: Deep reinforcement learning can be used to train self-driving cars to navigate roads and respond to different driving scenarios.
4. **Finance**: Deep reinforcement learning can be used in finance to optimize trading strategies and make investment decisions.
5. **Healthcare**: Deep reinforcement learning can be used in healthcare to optimize treatment plans and predict patient outcomes.

Example of Deep Reinforcement Learning in Action One example of deep reinforcement learning in action is the development of AlphaGo, an AI system developed by Google DeepMind to play the game of Go. AlphaGo uses a combination of deep neural networks and reinforcement learning to learn the complex strategies involved in playing Go.

Through a process of trial and error, AlphaGo was able to learn from its mistakes and improve its performance over time. In 2016, AlphaGo made history by defeating the world champion at Go in a five-game match.

Conclusion

In this chapter, we've explored the exciting field of deep reinforcement learning and its applications in AI projects. We've discussed the combination of deep learning and reinforcement learning and provided examples of how deep reinforcement learning can be used in projects such as robotics, gaming, self-driving cars, finance, and healthcare.

Remember, deep reinforcement learning is a powerful tool for building complex AI systems. By understanding the principles of deep reinforcement learning and its applications, you can identify new opportunities for implementing AI in your projects and stay ahead of the curve in the rapidly evolving field of AI.

Chapter 12: What is Explainable AI and How Can It Be Used in Projects?

Welcome to Chapter 12 of "The Roadmap to AI Mastery: A Guide to Building and Scaling Projects." In this chapter, we'll explore the concept of explainable AI and its applications in AI projects.

What is Explainable AI?

Explainable AI (XAI) is a subfield of AI that involves building AI systems that can explain their decision-making processes in a way that is understandable to humans. This is important for ensuring transparency and accountability in AI systems.

Traditional AI systems, such as deep neural networks, can be difficult to interpret and understand. This can be problematic in situations where the consequences of AI decisions are significant, such as in healthcare or finance.

Explainable AI involves building AI systems that can provide insight into how they arrive at their decisions, making them more transparent and understandable.

How Can Explainable AI Be Used in Projects?

Explainable AI can be used in a wide range of AI projects, including:

1. *Healthcare*: Explainable AI can be used in healthcare to help doctors and other medical professionals understand the reasoning behind an AI diagnosis or treatment recommendation.
2. *Finance*: Explainable AI can be used in finance to help traders and investors understand the reasoning behind an AI investment recommendation.
3. *Fraud Detection*: Explainable AI can be used in fraud detection to help investigators understand the reasoning behind an AI system's determination that a transaction is fraudulent.
4. *Customer Service*: Explainable AI can be used in customer service to help customers understand the reasoning behind an AI system's response to a support inquiry.

Example of Explainable AI in Action

One example of explainable AI in action is IBM's Watson for Oncology system. Watson for Oncology is an AI system designed to help doctors make treatment recommendations for cancer patients.

The system uses natural language processing and machine learning to analyze patient data and provide treatment recommendations. However, to ensure transparency and accountability, Watson for Oncology also provides an explanation for each recommendation it makes, including a list of the evidence and data used to support the recommendation.

This explanation helps doctors understand the reasoning behind each recommendation and make informed decisions about patient care.

Conclusion

In this chapter, we've explored the concept of explainable AI and its applications in AI projects. We've discussed the importance of transparency and accountability in AI systems and provided examples of how explainable AI can be used in healthcare, finance, fraud detection, and customer service.

Remember, explainable AI is a powerful tool for building transparent and accountable AI systems. By understanding the principles of explainable AI and its applications, you can identify new opportunities for implementing AI in your projects and ensure that your AI systems are transparent and understandable to humans.

Chapter 13: What is Federated Learning and How Can It Be Used in Projects?

Welcome to Chapter 13 of "The Roadmap to AI Mastery: A Guide to Building and Scaling Projects." In this chapter, we'll explore the concept of federated learning and its applications in AI projects.

What is Federated Learning?

Federated learning is a distributed machine learning approach that allows multiple parties to collaboratively train a model without sharing their data. This can help address privacy concerns while still allowing for the development of accurate models.

In traditional machine learning, data is collected and stored in a central location, and models are trained on this data. This approach can raise privacy concerns, particularly when the data being used is sensitive or confidential.

Federated learning involves training models on data that remains stored locally on individual devices or servers, without sharing the data itself. This allows multiple parties to collaborate on training the model without exposing sensitive data to unauthorized access.

How Can Federated Learning Be Used in Projects?

Federated learning can be used in a wide range of AI projects, including:

1. ***Healthcare***: Federated learning can be used in healthcare to train models on patient data from multiple hospitals or clinics, without sharing the data itself.
2. ***Finance***: Federated learning can be used in finance to train models on financial data from multiple institutions, without sharing the data itself.
3. ***Internet of Things***: Federated learning can be used in the Internet of Things (IoT) to train models on data collected from multiple devices, without sharing the data itself.
4. ***Advertising***: Federated learning can be used in advertising to train models on user data from multiple sources, without sharing the data itself.

Example of Federated Learning in Action

One example of federated learning in action is Google's Federated Learning of Cohorts (FLoC) project. FLoC is a privacy-preserving advertising technology that allows advertisers to target groups of users with similar interests without revealing individual user data.

FLoC uses federated learning to train models on user data from individual devices, without sharing the data itself. This allows advertisers to target groups of users based on their interests, while maintaining user privacy.

Conclusion

In this chapter, we've explored the concept of federated learning and its applications in AI projects. We've discussed the importance of privacy and security in AI systems and provided examples of how federated learning can be used in healthcare, finance, IoT, and advertising.

Remember, federated learning is a powerful tool for building accurate models while maintaining data privacy and security.

By understanding the principles of federated learning and its applications, you can identify new opportunities for implementing AI in your projects and ensure that your AI systems maintain the privacy and security of sensitive data.

Chapter 14: What is Generative Adversarial Networks and How Can It Be Used in Projects?

Welcome to Chapter 14 of "The Roadmap to AI Mastery: A Guide to Building and Scaling Projects." In this chapter, we'll explore the concept of Generative Adversarial Networks (GANs) and its applications in AI projects.

What are Generative Adversarial Networks?

Generative Adversarial Networks (GANs) are a type of neural network that can generate new data based on existing data. GANs work by using two neural networks: a generator network and a discriminator network.

The generator network is trained to generate new data that is similar to the existing data. The discriminator network is trained to distinguish between the generated data and the real data.

The two networks are trained together in a process called adversarial training. The generator network tries to create data that can fool the discriminator network, while the discriminator network tries to correctly identify the real data. This process continues until the generator network is able to create data that is indistinguishable from the real data.

How Can Generative Adversarial Networks Be Used in Projects?

Generative Adversarial Networks can be used in a wide range of AI projects, including:

1. ***Art and Music Generation***: GANs can be used to generate new pieces of art or music based on existing pieces.
2. ***Image and Video Synthesis***: GANs can be used to generate new images or videos that are similar to existing images or videos.
3. ***Data Augmentation***: GANs can be used to generate new data for training AI models, improving model accuracy.
4. ***Video Game Development***: GANs can be used to generate new levels or characters for video games.

Example of Generative Adversarial Networks in Action

One example of GANs in action is the StyleGAN2 model developed by Nvidia. StyleGAN2 is a GAN-based model that can generate new human faces that are almost indistinguishable from real human faces.

The model works by using a dataset of real human faces to train the generator and discriminator networks. The generator network then generates new faces that are evaluated by the discriminator network. This process continues until the generator network is able to create faces that are indistinguishable from the real faces.

Conclusion

In this chapter, we've explored the concept of Generative Adversarial Networks (GANs) and its applications in AI projects. We've discussed the process of adversarial training and provided examples of how GANs can be used in art and music generation, image and video synthesis, data augmentation, and video game development.

Remember, GANs are a powerful tool for generating new data based on existing data. By understanding the principles of GANs and their applications, you can identify new opportunities for implementing AI in your projects and create new data that can improve model accuracy and performance.

Chapter 15: What is Edge Computing and How Can It Be Used in Projects?

Welcome to Chapter 15 of "The Roadmap to AI Mastery: A Guide to Building and Scaling Projects." In this chapter, we'll explore the concept of edge computing and its applications in AI projects.

What is Edge Computing?

Edge computing is a distributed computing approach that brings computation and data storage closer to the devices and sensors that generate the data. This can help reduce latency, increase data privacy, and improve network efficiency.

In traditional computing, data is processed and stored in a centralized location such as a data center or cloud. This approach can be problematic when dealing with large amounts of data generated by sensors and devices in real-time.

Edge computing involves processing and storing data locally on devices or at the network edge, such as on a local server or gateway. This allows for real-time processing and analysis of data, without the need to transfer the data to a centralized location.

How Can Edge Computing Be Used in Projects?

Edge computing can be used in a wide range of AI projects, including:

1. ***Industrial IoT***: Edge computing can be used in industrial IoT applications to enable real-time monitoring and control of equipment and processes.
2. ***Smart Cities***: Edge computing can be used in smart cities to enable real-time analysis and optimization of traffic flow, energy usage, and other municipal services.
3. ***Healthcare***: Edge computing can be used in healthcare to enable real-time monitoring and analysis of patient data, improving patient outcomes.
4. ***Autonomous Vehicles***: Edge computing can be used in autonomous vehicles to enable real-time analysis of sensor data and decision-making for safe and efficient driving.

Example of Edge Computing in Action

One example of edge computing in action is the Amazon Web Services (AWS) Greengrass platform. AWS Greengrass is a software platform that enables edge computing for IoT devices.

With AWS Greengrass, IoT devices can perform local computation and data storage, without relying on cloud-based services. This allows for real-time processing and analysis of data, improving response times and reducing network traffic.

Conclusion

In this chapter, we've explored the concept of edge computing and its applications in AI projects. We've discussed the benefits of edge computing, including reduced latency, increased data privacy, and improved network efficiency, and provided examples of how edge computing can be used in industrial IoT, smart cities, healthcare, and autonomous vehicles.

Remember, edge computing is a powerful tool for enabling real-time processing and analysis of data. By understanding the principles of edge computing and its applications, you can identify new opportunities for implementing AI in your projects and improve the performance and efficiency of your AI systems.

Chapter 16: What is Embedded Machine Learning and How is it Different from Federated Learning?

Welcome to Chapter 16 of "The Roadmap to AI Mastery: A Guide to Building and Scaling Projects." In this chapter, we'll explore the concept of embedded machine learning and its applications in AI projects, and we'll compare it with federated learning.

What is Embedded Machine Learning?

Embedded machine learning is a type of machine learning that involves running machine learning algorithms on small, low-power devices, such as smartphones or IoT sensors. The goal of embedded machine learning is to enable real-time, on-device decision-making without the need for cloud-based processing.

Embedded machine learning algorithms are typically optimized for low-power consumption and limited computing resources. This can involve techniques such as model compression, where the model size is reduced, and quantization, where the model parameters are represented using fewer bits.

How is Embedded Machine Learning Different from Federated Learning?

Embedded machine learning and federated learning are both distributed machine learning approaches, but they differ in several keyways.

Federated learning involves training models on data that remains stored locally on individual devices or servers, without sharing the data itself. This allows multiple parties to collaborate on training the model without exposing sensitive data to unauthorized access.

Embedded machine learning, on the other hand, involves running machine learning algorithms directly on small, low-power devices, without the need for cloud-based processing.

While both approaches enable real-time, on-device decision-making, embedded machine learning is typically used for individual devices, while federated learning is used for collaborative training on multiple devices.

How Can Embedded Machine Learning Be Used in Projects?

Embedded machine learning can be used in a wide range of AI projects, including:

1. ***Smart Home Automation***: Embedded machine learning can be used in smart home automation to enable real-time analysis and control of devices, such as lighting or temperature control.
2. ***Healthcare***: Embedded machine learning can be used in healthcare to enable real-time monitoring and analysis of patient data, such as heart rate or blood pressure.
3. ***Autonomous Vehicles***: Embedded machine learning can be used in autonomous vehicles to enable real-time analysis of sensor data and decision-making for safe and efficient driving.
4. ***Industrial IoT***: Embedded machine learning can be used in industrial IoT applications to enable real-time monitoring and control of equipment and processes.

Example of Embedded Machine Learning in Action

One example of embedded machine learning in action is the Google Pixel 4 smartphone. The Pixel 4 uses on-device machine learning to power features such as facial recognition and real-time transcription of voice notes.

The Pixel 4 includes a machine learning chip, called the Pixel Neural Core, that enables efficient on-device processing of machine learning algorithms. This allows for real-time, on-device decision-making without the need for cloud-based processing.

Conclusion

In this chapter, we've explored the concept of embedded machine learning and its applications in AI projects. We've discussed the benefits of embedded machine learning, including real-time, on-device decision-making and reduced dependence on cloud-based processing, and provided examples of how embedded machine learning can be used in smart home automation, healthcare, autonomous vehicles, and industrial IoT.

Remember, embedded machine learning is a powerful tool for enabling real-time decision-making on small, low-power devices. By understanding the principles of embedded machine learning and its applications, you can identify new opportunities for implementing AI in your projects and improve the performance and efficiency of your AI systems.

Chapter 17: How AI can be used to promote Environmental, Social, and Corporate Governance (ESG)

Welcome to Chapter 17 of "The Roadmap to AI Mastery: A Guide to Building and Scaling Projects." In this chapter, we'll explore how AI can be used to promote Environmental, Social, and Corporate Governance (ESG).

What is ESG?

Environmental, Social, and Corporate Governance (ESG) is a framework for assessing the sustainability and ethical impact of business practices. ESG considerations cover a wide range of factors, including environmental impact, social responsibility, and corporate governance.

ESG has become an increasingly important consideration for businesses, investors, and consumers, as they seek to promote sustainable and responsible practices.

How can AI be used to promote ESG?

AI can be used in a wide range of applications to promote ESG, including:

1. *Environmental Sustainability*: AI can be used to monitor and analyze environmental data, such as air quality or water pollution, enabling more efficient and effective resource management.
2. *Social Responsibility*: AI can be used to analyze social data, such as customer feedback or social

media sentiment, to inform responsible business practices and decision-making.
3. *Corporate Governance*: AI can be used to monitor and analyze corporate data, such as financial records or executive compensation, to ensure compliance with ethical and legal standards.

Example of AI in Promoting ESG

One example of AI in promoting ESG is the use of machine learning algorithms to monitor and analyze air quality data. Companies such as Aclima and Plume Labs have developed sensors and AI algorithms that can detect air pollutants in real-time and provide recommendations for reducing exposure to harmful pollutants.

Another example is the use of natural language processing (NLP) to analyze customer feedback and social media sentiment. Companies such as IBM and Microsoft have developed NLP algorithms that can detect patterns and trends in customer feedback, enabling businesses to identify areas for improvement and promote responsible business practices.

Conclusion

In this chapter, we've explored how AI can be used to promote Environmental, Social, and Corporate Governance (ESG). We've discussed the importance of ESG considerations for businesses, investors, and consumers, and provided examples of how AI can be used to promote environmental sustainability, social responsibility, and corporate governance.

Remember, AI can be a powerful tool for promoting ESG, but it's important to use it in a responsible and ethical manner. By understanding the principles of ESG and its applications in AI, you can identify new opportunities for implementing AI in your projects and promoting sustainable and responsible business practices.

Chapter 18: How AI can be used to promote Environmental Sustainability

Welcome to Chapter 18 of "The Roadmap to AI Mastery: A Guide to Building and Scaling Projects." In this chapter, we'll explore how AI can be used to promote environmental sustainability.

What is Environmental Sustainability?

Environmental sustainability is the practice of using resources in a way that meets the needs of the present generation without compromising the ability of future generations to meet their own needs. It involves reducing waste, conserving resources, and minimizing the impact of human activities on the environment.

How Can AI be used to Promote Environmental Sustainability?

AI can be used in a wide range of applications to promote environmental sustainability, including:

1. *Energy Efficiency*: AI can be used to optimize energy usage in buildings and industrial processes, reducing waste and lowering greenhouse gas emissions.
2. *Waste Management*: AI can be used to optimize waste management processes, such as recycling and composting, to reduce the amount of waste sent to landfills and promote sustainable resource usage.

3. ***Agriculture and Food Production***: AI can be used to improve crop yields, reduce pesticide usage, and optimize food distribution, reducing food waste and promoting sustainable food systems.

Example of AI in Promoting Environmental Sustainability

One example of AI in promoting environmental sustainability is the use of machine learning algorithms to reduce food waste and hunger around the world. The company Nosh Technologies has developed an AI-powered platform that uses embedded machine learning to understand food consumption and wastage in different regions of the world. The platform then uses this data to help optimize food waste.

Nosh Technologies has partnered with consumers, food banks, retailers and other organizations to manage food more effectively. The platform also provides data and insights to consumers, businesses and policymakers to inform sustainable food policies and reduce food waste.

Another example is the use of AI in energy efficiency. Companies such as Honeywell and Siemens have developed AI-powered building management systems that optimize energy usage based on real-time data and occupancy patterns. These systems can help reduce energy waste and lower greenhouse gas emissions.

Conclusion

In this chapter, we've explored how AI can be used to promote environmental sustainability. We've discussed the importance of environmental sustainability for preserving resources for future generations, and provided examples of how AI can be used to promote sustainable practices in energy efficiency, waste management, and agriculture and food production.

Remember, AI can be a powerful tool for promoting environmental sustainability, but it's important to use it in a responsible and ethical manner. By understanding the principles of environmental sustainability and its applications in AI, you can identify new opportunities for implementing AI in your projects and promoting sustainable practices in your organization.

Bonus Chapter: How to Communicate Effectively with Technical People in AI

Welcome to the Bonus Chapter of "The Roadmap to AI Mastery: A Guide to Building and Scaling Projects." In this chapter, we'll explore how to communicate effectively with technical people in AI, an essential skill for any project or product manager working on AI projects.

Communicating effectively with technical people can be a challenge, especially if you have a non-technical background. Technical people may use jargon, acronyms, and technical terms that are unfamiliar to you, making it difficult to understand their ideas and explain your own. However, effective communication is essential to building successful AI projects that meet your organization's business goals.

Here are some tips for communicating effectively with technical people in AI:

1. *Be clear and concise*: Avoid using jargon or technical terms that may be unfamiliar to your audience. Use simple, easy-to-understand language and explain concepts in a clear and concise manner. Use examples and analogies to help illustrate your point.
2. *Listen actively*: Take the time to listen to technical people and ask questions to clarify any concepts or terms that you may not understand. Active listening shows that you value their input and can help you better understand their ideas.

3. ***Ask for feedback***: After explaining your ideas, ask technical people for their feedback and opinions. This can help you identify any gaps or misunderstandings in your communication and lead to better collaboration and more effective project outcomes.
4. ***Learn the basics***: While you don't need to become a technical expert, it's helpful to have a basic understanding of AI concepts and terminology. This can help you better understand technical people's ideas and communicate your own effectively.

Example of Effective Communication with Technical People in AI

One example of effective communication with technical people in AI is the partnership between Google and the University of Michigan to develop an AI-powered healthcare tool. The team was made up of researchers, engineers, and clinicians, each with different backgrounds and areas of expertise.

To ensure effective communication, the team used a "plain language" approach to explain technical concepts and ideas to non-technical team members. They also used visual aids, such as diagrams and flowcharts, to help illustrate complex ideas and processes.

As a result of their effective communication, the team was able to build a successful AI-powered tool that helps clinicians identify patients at risk of developing certain medical conditions, leading to better patient outcomes.

Conclusion

In this Bonus Chapter, we've explored how to communicate effectively with technical people in AI, an essential skill for any project or product manager working on AI projects. By being clear and concise, listening actively, asking for feedback, and learning the basics, you can better understand technical people's ideas and communicate your own effectively.

Remember, effective communication is essential to building successful AI projects that meet your organization's business goals. By following these tips and using real-world examples, you can become a more effective communicator and a better collaborator with technical people in AI.

Bonus Chapter: How to Communicate Effectively with Non-Technical People About AI Projects

Welcome to the Bonus Chapter of "The Roadmap to AI Mastery: A Guide to Building and Scaling Projects." In this chapter, we'll explore how to communicate effectively with non-technical people about AI projects, an essential skill for any project or product manager working on AI projects.

Communicating effectively with non-technical people can be a challenge, especially when it comes to AI, which can be complex and difficult to understand. However, effective communication is essential to building successful AI projects that meet your organization's business goals.

Here are some tips for communicating effectively with non-technical people about AI projects:

1. *Use plain language*: Avoid using jargon or technical terms that may be unfamiliar to your audience. Use simple, easy-to-understand language and explain concepts in a clear and concise manner. Use examples and analogies to help illustrate your point.
2. *Focus on the benefits*: Non-technical people may not be interested in the technical details of AI projects, but they will be interested in how it can benefit their business. Focus on the benefits of the project, such as improved efficiency, cost savings, or better customer experiences.

3. *Use visual aids*: Visual aids, such as diagrams, flowcharts, or infographics, can help explain complex ideas and processes in a way that is easy to understand. Use them to help illustrate your point and make your presentation more engaging.
4. *Be patient*: Non-technical people may need more time to understand complex ideas and processes. Be patient, answer questions, and provide additional resources, such as articles or videos, to help them better understand the project.

Example of Effective Communication with Non-Technical People About AI Projects

One example of effective communication with non-technical people about AI projects is the partnership between Uber and Carnegie Mellon University to develop autonomous vehicles. The project involved complex AI algorithms and technology, but Uber's CEO, Travis Kalanick, knew that he needed to communicate the benefits of the project to non-technical stakeholders, such as investors and policymakers.

To do this, Kalanick focused on the benefits of autonomous vehicles, such as reduced traffic congestion, improved safety, and increased accessibility for people who cannot drive. He used visual aids, such as videos of autonomous vehicles in action, to help illustrate the benefits and create a compelling vision for the future.

As a result of his effective communication, Kalanick was able to secure $1 billion in funding for the project and build support among policymakers for the development of autonomous vehicles.

Conclusion

In this Bonus Chapter, we've explored how to communicate effectively with non-technical people about AI projects, an essential skill for any project or product manager working on AI projects. By using plain language, focusing on the benefits, using visual aids, and being patient, you can better communicate the benefits of AI projects to non-technical stakeholders.

Remember, effective communication is essential to building successful AI projects that meet your organization's business goals. By following these tips and using real-world examples, you can become a more effective communicator and build support for AI projects among non-technical stakeholders.

Thank You for Reading

Welcome to Chapter 19 of "The Roadmap to AI Mastery: A Guide to Building and Scaling Projects." In this final chapter, we want to take a moment to thank you, our readers, for taking the time to read this book.

We hope that the content of this book has been informative, engaging, and helpful in your journey to build and scale AI projects that promote your company's business goals.

Throughout this book, we've explored a wide range of topics, from understanding the fundamentals of AI to selecting the right framework, creating AI models, and overcoming common challenges. We've also explored emerging technologies and trends in AI, and discussed how AI can be used to promote environmental sustainability and ESG.

We've provided detailed examples, practical tips, and friendly advice to help you navigate the complex world of AI and build successful projects that meet your organization's needs. We hope that the knowledge and skills you've gained from reading this book will help you achieve your goals and contribute to the growth and success of your company.

At the heart of this book is our commitment to making AI accessible, understandable, and approachable for everyone. We believe that AI has the potential to transform industries, improve people's lives, and make the world a better place. But we also know that AI can be complex, intimidating, and difficult to navigate.

That's why we've written this book in a friendly tone, using real-world examples and practical advice to demystify AI and make it more accessible for everyone.

In closing, we want to express our gratitude to you, our readers, for taking the time to read this book. We hope that the knowledge and skills you've gained from reading this book will serve you well in your journey to build and scale AI projects.

We also want to encourage you to continue learning, exploring, and experimenting with AI. The world of AI is constantly evolving, and there are always new opportunities and challenges to explore.

Thank you for joining us on this journey, and we wish you all the best in your future endeavours.

Connect with the author

Hope the contents from this book have helped you to gain fundamental introductory understanding of AI and helped you to build and scale AI projects within your company. I often post related contents on AI development on my social media channels as follows:

LinkedIn: http://linkedin.com/in/somdipdey

Facebook: http://facebook.com/deysomdip

Koo: http://kooapp.com/profile/somdipdey

Let's stay in touch and help each other to build AI projects that matters!

www.ingramcontent.com/pod-product-compliance
Lightning Source LLC
Chambersburg PA
CBHW030453220526
45464CB00006B/2514